How to Be President of the U.S.A.

by Murray Suid

Illustrated by Marilynn G. Barr

This book is for
Leslie Tryon
and
Jay Fowler

Publisher: Roberta Suid
Editor: Jeffrey Goldman
Design: David Hale
Copy Editor: Carol Whiteley
Production: Santa Monica Press
Consultants: Sue Krumbein and Phyllis McCarthy

Other books by the author: *Book Factory, Editing,
Greeting Cards, Letter Writing, More Book Factory,
Picture Book Factory, Report Factory, Research,
Sentences, Stories, Writing Hangups, Ten-Minute
Thinking Tie-ins, Ten-Minute Whole Language Warm-ups*

Monday Morning is a registered trademark of
Monday Morning Books, Inc.

ISBN 1-878279-47-5

Printed in the United States of America

9 8 7 6 5 4 3

CONTENTS

INTRODUCTION

Presidents aren't born: they're made. Exactly how, no one knows. But clearly most of our successful leaders mastered the kind of how-to-do-it information found in this book.

The following pages present dozens of activities, each designed to help readers learn facts or sharpen skills that Presidents, and all citizens, should know.

The activities take various forms including checklists, fill-ins, quizzes, and interviews. Often, follow-up resource pages provide answers, enrichment information, writing models, or historic materials. Numerous bonus projects aim to take readers into the real world, for example, by polling neighbors and interviewing local leaders.

The book has six parts:

- *Learn the Basics* outlines the Chief Executive's job and relates it to the Constitution.

- *Get Ready* highlights skills and knowledge all leaders need, for example, a good memory.

- *Get Elected* presents strategies for campaigning.

- *Take Office* covers inauguration happenings, as well as facts about the White House and Washington, D.C.

- *Go to Work* explains the major tasks every President faces, from shaping laws to handling crises.

- *Leave Office* deals with what Presidents do after moving out of the White House and returning to private life. Here, you'll also find famous quotations and pictures of the Presidents.

A detailed index should make it easier to track down speeches and other historic items that are scattered throughout the book. Two examples are Grace Bedell's famous letter suggesting that Abe Lincoln grow a beard, and Ronald Reagan's inspiring message concerning the *Challenger* space shuttle disaster.

An annotated Reading List and a Presidential Address Book provide additional resources for those who want to dig a little deeper.

We hope this book will inspire readers to become active, intelligent participants in the ongoing democratic experiment known as the United States of America. While not everyone can become President, all of us can be devoted Americans.

LEARN THE BASICS

*The Executive power shall be vested in a
President of the United States of America.*
Constitution of The United States
March 4, 1789

DEFINE LEADERSHIP

A scientist must be curious, and a weight lifter needs to be strong. But people don't agree on what makes a good President. For example, some say that a leader should be open-minded. Yet several of our best Presidents have been stubborn.

Try this: *Check the words you think describe a good President. Add more if you like.*

☐ Brave

☐ Caring

☐ Cooperative

☐ Curious

☐ Energetic

☐ Friendly

☐ Gentle

☐ Hard-working

☐ Honest

☐ Smart

☐ _____

☐ _____

President Dwight Eisenhower's Checklist

Here's what Dwight Eisenhower looked for in a leader.

✓ Good values: For example, telling the truth.

✓ Understanding what makes our country great: Respecting people's freedom to work for themselves, their families, and their communities. The government shouldn't boss people around.

✓ Calmness: Being able to make good decisions when other people become confused because of fear.

✓ Strength of decision: Having enough confidence to seek strong advisors rather than people who only say what you want to hear.

✓ Experience: Being prepared by past challenges to handle crises.

✓ Character: Doing what's right, not what's easy. Refusing to run away when the going gets tough.

Bonus: *Take a poll. Ask people what they look for in a leader. You might also write to your town's mayor and other leaders, asking for their ideas. Compare the answers you get with the points you checked. Think about what you might do to make yourself a better leader.*

TAKE A PRESIDENTIAL QUIZ

Being President of the United States is one of the world's most important jobs. Maybe someday that job will be yours. Here's a chance to find out how much you already know about it.

Try this: *Decide if the following statements are "True" or "False."*

	TRUE	FALSE
1. The President must be a man.	☐	☐
2. The President must obey the law, just like everyone else.	☐	☐
3. The President has to be married.	☐	☐
4. The President must be at least 35 years old.	☐	☐
5. Only a person who is a citizen at birth can be elected President of the United States.	☐	☐
6. You can be elected President even if you don't know how to read.	☐	☐
7. The President must be a lawyer.	☐	☐
8. The President cannot be deaf or blind or have any physical handicap.	☐	☐
9. The President must have had military experience.	☐	☐
10. A person can be elected President only twice.	☐	☐
11. The President must earn more money than anyone else in the country.	☐	☐

★PRESIDENTIAL QUIZ ANSWERS★

1. FALSE. While there has never been a female President of the United States, by law a woman can be President. In other countries, such as England, India, and Israel, women have served as head of state. In the U.S. many women have run for President, backed by minor parties. Examples are: Victoria Woodhull, Equal Rights Party (1872); Charlene Mitchell, Communist Party (1968); Margaret Smith, Peace and Freedom Party (1980); and Ellen McCormack, Right to Life Party (1980). In 1984, Geraldine Ferraro, a Congresswoman, became the first female from a major party to run for Vice President.

2. TRUE. For example, a President who is convicted of a serious crime, such as treason or bribery, will be removed from office. The first step in this process is called "impeachment." Andrew Johnson is the only President who has ever been impeached. None has been convicted and removed from office. Richard Nixon, when threatened with impeachment, left office voluntarily.

3. FALSE. But only one President, James Buchanan, stayed a bachelor.

4. TRUE. As of 1991, the youngest President was Theodore Roosevelt, who was 42 when he took office. The oldest was Ronald Reagan, 69.

5. TRUE. A person born in another country qualifies if at least one parent is a citizen of the United States and has lived in the U.S. People who are not natural-born citizens may hold important jobs such as Secretary of State.

6. TRUE. The Constitution doesn't mention education. Nine Presidents did not attend college, including Washington, Lincoln, and Truman.

7. FALSE. While over half of the Presidents have had law degrees or have at least studied law, those who didn't include Washington, Grant, Wilson, Hoover, Eisenhower, Kennedy, Carter, and Reagan.

8. FALSE. For example, Franklin Roosevelt spent much time in a wheelchair. However, if a handicap or injury keeps a President from working, the President may be removed from office.

9. FALSE. Though the President is Commander in Chief, the Constitution doesn't require prior military experience. However, many Presidents have served in the armed forces. A dozen reached the rank of general.

10. TRUE. Before the passage of the 22nd Amendment (1951), a President could be elected again and again, though only Franklin Roosevelt won office more than twice. Today, the limit is two electoral wins plus two years completing another President's term. A person who serves more than two years of another President's term may be elected only once.

11. FALSE. In 1992, the President earned $200,000 a year plus $170,000 to cover travel, entertainment, and other expenses. Thousands of people earn more than this.

STUDY THE CONSTITUTION

The U.S.A. isn't just a place. It's an *idea* that people should control the government, and not the other way around. This idea is outlined in the Constitution, the nation's basic law. On the day you become President, you promise to "preserve, protect and defend" the Constitution. Before you move into the White House, learn all you can about this important law.

Try this: *Give extra attention to the Bill of Rights. This part of the Constitution lists rights that the United States government can't take away from the people or the states.*

Take a poll. Use tally marks (卌) to show how many people agree or disagree with some of the freedoms found in the Bill of Rights. You might report what you learn in your school or local paper.

BILL OF RIGHTS POLL

	AGREE	DISAGREE
1. Congress shouldn't make laws telling people which religion to follow or not to follow.		
2. Congress should not limit the freedoms of speech or the press.		
3. People should have the right to ask the government to correct problems.		
4. Because military forces are needed to maintain freedom, people should have the right to keep and carry weapons.		
5. The government shouldn't search a person or a person's house without a warrant (legal paper from a judge).		
6. People shouldn't be forced to be witnesses against themselves in a trial.		
7. People accused of a crime should have the right to a jury trial, and the right to have a lawyer.		

★STORY OF THE CONSTITUTION★

Long ago, most countries were ruled by a strong king or queen. The leader's word was law. People had few rights and took no part in the government. A country's soldiers might even be used against its own people if they complained.

Most Americans who took part in the Revolutionary War hated all-powerful leaders. In 1787, the 13 original states sent 55 delegates to Philadelphia to create a new country: the United States. They wanted a nation in which laws would be made by the people. The leaders would have to obey the laws just like everyone else.

To make this dream come true, James Madison, Alexander Hamilton, and other planners wrote a set of rules called the Constitution. Just as the rules of a game tell how to play, the Constitution tells how to run the country. Among other things, the Constitution explains:

- Why the United States should exist

- How laws will be made and who will make them

- How the President will be chosen and what the President will do

- How judges are picked and what the courts will do

The Constitution divides the government into three parts (branches).

The *legislative branch* (Congress) makes the laws. This branch is made up of both the Senate and the House of Representatives.

The *executive branch* sees that the laws are followed. This branch is headed by the President.

The *judicial branch* (the Supreme Court and other federal courts) makes sure that the laws and trials are fair.

Each branch has some power over the other branches. This way, no single person or group can take over the government and threaten to take away the people's freedom.

Those who wrote the Constitution knew that it wasn't perfect. For this reason, they included rules on how to change and improve the Constitution.

This is a very important idea. For example, in 1789, when George Washington became the first President of the United States, only white men were allowed to vote. Years later, citizens saw that such a rule made no sense. They changed (amended) the Constitution to give women and people of all races equal rights under the law.

INTERVIEW A LEADER

Leadership is a skill that can be practiced in many jobs. For example, before becoming President of the United States, George Washington was Commander in Chief of the Continental Army. Dwight Eisenhower was a World War II general and later became the head of Columbia University.

Try this: *To learn about leadership, interview a leader. He or she might be:*

- Your town's mayor

- The head of your school's parent-teacher group

- The school principal

- The manager of a sports team

- The owner of a business

- A religious leader

Ask the person what it takes to be a leader. Talk about the good and bad parts of the job. Write your interview as a report or for your school paper.

Bonus: *Write an imaginary interview with a President. Start with library research. Look for books with presidential letters and speeches, plus such resources as <u>Bartlett's Familiar Quotations</u>. Present the interview as a two-person play.*

Tips for Interviewing

1. Read newspaper and magazine interviews to learn about asking good questions.

2. Set up a time to meet the person you want to interview. You'll need about 30 minutes.

3. Before doing the interview, write ten questions you plan to ask.

4. Begin the interview with fact questions about the person's educational background, birthplace, and so on.

5. As the person talks, write down the important words. Skip "ums" and "ers." If you can't write fast enough, ask the person to slow down. Or use a tape recorder if the person agrees.

6. When you write up your interview, begin with a short introduction that describes the person's background.

★IMAGINARY INTERVIEW★

Harry S. Truman, the 33rd President of the United States, was born May 8, 1884, in Lamar, Missouri. He claimed he had read every book in his local library by the time he was fourteen.

He worked for a railroad, a bank, and on his family's farm. He volunteered for service in World War I. After the war, he married his childhood sweetheart Bess, and started a men's store.

Later, voters chose him to supervise the building of roads. In 1934, he won election to the United States Senate. In 1944, President Roosevelt asked him to run as Vice President. When Roosevelt died, Truman took over.

Here is part of an imaginary interview in which President Truman talks about running the country. It uses his actual words, as found in quotation books.

QUESTION: How did you feel when you learned you were going to be President?

TRUMAN: Like the moon, the stars, and all the planets had fallen on me.

QUESTION: So why didn't you just quit?

TRUMAN: A leader has to lead, or otherwise, he has no business in politics. If you can't stand the heat, get out of the kitchen.

QUESTION: But do you really think one person can make a difference?

TRUMAN: In periods where there is no leadership, society stands still. Progress occurs when courageous, skillful leaders . . . change things for the better.

QUESTION: But what if people don't like what you're doing? What if they say mean things about you?

TRUMAN: If somebody throws a brick at me, I can catch it and throw it back. But when somebody awards a decoration to me, I am out of words.

QUESTION: We're just about out of time. Can you sum up the President's job in just a few words?

TRUMAN: The buck [responsibility] stops here.

PART 2

GET READY

If a nation expects to be ignorant and free, in a state of civilization, it expects what never was and never will be.
Thomas Jefferson
January 6, 1816

LEARN TO WORK

Running a country isn't easy. Presidents work many hours, often on weekends. During one day, tasks might include:

- Writing letters
- Meeting a foreign leader
- Working on a budget
- Giving a speech

Where do Presidents get the skills to do so much? A clue is that most of them held many jobs before reaching the White House. On the way to the presidency, our leaders have done everything from acting in Hollywood movies to running clothing stores.

Try this: *List three jobs that you would like to have before becoming President. Tell how you think these jobs would prepare you for leadership. For example, being a lion tamer might make you brave.*

FUTURE JOBS

1) _____

2) _____

3) _____

Bonus: *List several chores you do around the house and explain how they might help you get ready to be President.*

Theodore Roosevelt's Pre-Presidential Jobs

Writer
Cowboy
Police commissioner
Assistant Secretary of the Navy
State assembly member
Soldier
Governor
Vice President

★PRE-PRESIDENTIAL JOBS★

Actor: Reagan

Architect: Jefferson

Banker: Coolidge

Bookkeeper: Truman

Builder: Garfield

Cabinet member: many Presidents

Charity director: Hoover

Clothmaker: Fillmore

Congressperson: many Presidents

Diplomat: many Presidents

District attorney: Cleveland

Engineer: Hoover

Farm owner/manager: Carter

Farmer: Truman

Football coach: Eisenhower

Governor: many Presidents

Horse breeder: Washington

Insurance agent: Harding

Inventor: Jefferson

Judge: many Presidents

Land speculator: Jackson

Lawyer: many Presidents

Mayor: many Presidents

Men's store owner: Truman

Mill hand: Fillmore, Lincoln

Miner: Hoover

Minister: Garfield

Musician: Harding

Newspaper editor: Harding

Oil business executive: Bush

Plantation owner: Washington, Jefferson

Postmaster: Lincoln

Printer's devil (helper): Harding

Rail splitter: Lincoln

Railroad timekeeper: Truman

Rancher: T. Roosevelt

Ranger: Ford

Reporter: Taft

Saloon owner: Lincoln

School principal: L. Johnson

Senator: many Presidents

Sheriff: Cleveland

Soldier: many Presidents

Sportscaster: Reagan

Steamboat pilot: Lincoln

Store clerk: Buchanan

Store manager: Lincoln

Surveyor: Washington, J. Adams, Lincoln

Tailor: A. Johnson

Tanner: Grant

Teacher: J.Q. Adams, Fillmore, Garfield

University president: Wilson, Eisenhower

KNOW WHAT'S GOING ON

As President, you'll meet and talk to all sorts of people, such as scientists, athletes, artists, teachers, truck drivers, students, soldiers, foreign visitors, musicians, inventors, and doctors.

Try this: *For each subject below, check a box to show how much you know. While no one expects you to be an expert on all subjects, you should try to find out more about current events.*

	KNOW A LOT	KNOW A LITTLE	NEED TO STUDY
Africa	☐	☐	☐
AIDS	☐	☐	☐
Air pollution	☐	☐	☐
Asia	☐	☐	☐
Baseball	☐	☐	☐
Black holes	☐	☐	☐
Dinosaurs	☐	☐	☐
Europe	☐	☐	☐
Fossil fuels	☐	☐	☐
Mars	☐	☐	☐
Mexico	☐	☐	☐
MTV	☐	☐	☐
Ozone layer	☐	☐	☐
Stock market	☐	☐	☐
United Nations	☐	☐	☐
Whales	☐	☐	☐

Bonus: *Whenever you learn about something that's new to you, write about it in a diary.*

KNOW THE LANDMARKS

A few places in the United States are so special, they have become national symbols. As President, you should be familiar with them.

Try this: *Name the following landmarks. If you can, tell where they are located and what makes them so important.*

1

2

3

4

5

6

7

8

9

Bonus: *Make a picture postcard for a landmark where you live. Share your card with a friend.*

★ AMERICAN LANDMARKS ANSWERS ★

1. GOLDEN GATE BRIDGE, San Francisco, CA: Built from 1933 to 1937, this is one of the world's longest and most beautiful suspension bridges. Designed by Joseph Strauss, for many years it symbolized the western "end" of the U.S.

2. GATEWAY ARCH, next to the Mississippi River, St. Louis, MO: This 630-foot stainless steel monument links the nation's east and west. It contains a museum honoring Lewis and Clark, two famous explorers of the west.

3. HOLLYWOOD SIGN, in the Hollywood Hills, Los Angeles, CA: These concrete letters symbolize the American motion picture industry, which came to Southern California in 1911.

4. KENNEDY SPACE CENTER at Cape Canaveral, FL: Begun in 1947, this is now the chief United States launch site for missiles and manned space flights.

5. LIBERTY BELL, Independence Hall, Philadelphia, PA: Originally hung in 1753, the bell rang on July 2, 1776, to celebrate the vote declaring the colonies' independence from England. During the Revolutionary War, it was hidden from the British in Allentown, PA. The bell cracked in 1835, was fixed, then cracked again in 1846.

6. MOUNT RUSHMORE, outside Keystone, SD: In 1927, Gutzon Borglum and his son began sculpting the 60-foot-high heads of Presidents Washington, Jefferson, Lincoln, and Theodore Roosevelt. They were finished 14 years later. In 1959, Alfred Hitchcock used a model of Mount Rushmore to film the climax of his movie, *North by Northwest*.

7. PLYMOUTH ROCK, Plymouth, MA: Pilgrims landed here on December 21, 1620, and founded the oldest European settlement in New England. Before leaving their ship, the colonists signed the "Mayflower Compact." This democratic agreement called for rule by the majority.

8. STATUE OF LIBERTY, Liberty (formerly Bedloe's) Island in New York Bay, near Manhattan: The copper statue, unveiled on October 28, 1886, by President Grover Cleveland, is 152 feet tall. This gift from France was made by Frederic Bartholdi. His mother was the model. A smaller version of the statue is located near the River Seine in Paris.

9. WHITE HOUSE, Washington, D.C.: The President's mansion was designed by James Hoban and built on a site chosen by George Washington, who never lived in it. When John Adams moved in, the place was not finished. Over the years, many Presidents have made changes to it.

KNOW THE WORDS

Some of our country's treasures are easy to see:

> *Oh, beautiful, for spacious skies,*
> *For amber waves of grain.*
> *For purple mountain majesties*
> *Above the fruited plain . . .*

Ideas are another kind of treasure that every President must know about.

Try this: *See if you can identify each famous quotation by drawing a line to the person, thing, or event it relates to.*

1. "Proclaim liberty throughout all the land . . ."

2. ". . . and that government of the people, by the people, for the people, shall not perish from the earth."

3. "I lift my lamp beside the golden door!"

4. "We, the people . . ."

5. "One if by land, and two if by sea."

6. ". . . all men are created equal."

7. "That's one small step for man; one giant leap for mankind."

8. ". . . give me liberty, or give me death!"

9. "I have a dream . . ."

10. "Ask not what your country can do for you, ask what you can do for your country."

A. Declaration of Independence

B. First message from the moon

C. Gettysburg Address

D. Liberty Bell

E. Patrick Henry

F. Martin Luther King, Jr.

G. Paul Revere's ride

H. United States Constitution

I. Statue of Liberty

J. John F. Kennedy

★KNOW THE WORDS ANSWERS★

1. D. Liberty Bell inscription: The words come from the Bible (Leviticus XXV, 10): "Proclaim liberty throughout all the land unto all the inhabitants thereof."

2. C. The Gettysburg Address, a speech made by Abraham Lincoln on November 19, 1863. Lincoln was dedicating a national cemetery at Gettysburg, PA. Some experts say that this is the most quoted speech of all time.

3. I. "The New Colossus" by Emma Lazarus, a poem engraved on the pedestal of the Statue of Liberty.

4. H. Preamble (introduction) to the Constitution of the United States: "We, the people of the United States, in order to form a more perfect Union, establish justice, insure domestic tranquility, provide for the common defense, promote the general welfare, and secure the blessings of liberty to ourselves and our posterity do ordain and establish this Constitution for the United States of America."

5. G. "Paul Revere's Ride" by Henry Wadsworth Longfellow. The words refer to the code that would tell how the British soldiers would move (by land or by sea) against the colonists.

6. A. Declaration of Independence by Thomas Jefferson. It was adopted by the Continental Congress in Philadelphia on July 4, 1776.

7. B. First message sent to earth by a person standing on the moon's surface. Spoken, July 21, 1969, by Neil Armstrong. Later, Armstrong and fellow astronaut Edwin Aldrin, Jr., set up a plaque that reads: "Here men from the planet Earth first set foot upon the Moon July 1969 A.D. We came in peace for all mankind."

8. E. Patrick Henry's speech to the Virginia Convention (March 23, 1775) urging the colony to join the rebellion against England.

9. F. Speech by Martin Luther King, Jr., delivered at the Civil Rights March on Washington, August 28, 1963: "I have a dream that one day on the red hills of Georgia the sons of former slaves and the sons of former slave owners will be able to sit down together at the table of brotherhood. I have a dream that my four little children will one day live in a nation where they will not be judged by the color of their skin, but by the content of their character. I have a dream that one day this nation will rise up and live out the true meaning of its creed: We hold these truths to be self-evident; that all men are created equal . . ."

10. J. John F. Kennedy's Inaugural Address, January 20, 1961.

KNOW AMERICA'S SYMBOLS

The Great Seal of the United States is a very important national symbol. It is used on treaties, the back of every dollar bill, and other official documents.

A version of the seal serves as the "Seal of the President of the United States." It appears on White House stationery and on the side of Air Force One, the President's jet.

When you are President, you will often use the seal, so you should understand what it means.

Try this: *See if you can answer questions about the seal.*

1. What bird is on the seal?

2. What kind of branch does the bird hold in its right talon? What does this branch stand for?

3. How many arrows does the bird hold in its left talon? What does this number stand for?

4. The Latin words "E Pluribus Unum" are printed on a banner held in the bird's beak. What do these words mean? Where else are these words used?

5. How many stars form the circle around the bird? What does this number stand for?

6. What is the bird wearing on its chest?

Bonus: *Learn about the symbols of your state. These might include its flag, seal, motto, official bird, and flower. Then draw a seal for your family. It could include an animal or a flower.*

★AMERICA'S SYMBOLS ANSWERS★

1. AN AMERICAN BALD EAGLE: This endangered species, a member of the hawk family, is the national bird. It wasn't Ben Franklin's favorite. In 1784 he wrote to a friend: "I wish the bald eagle had not been chosen as the Representative of our Country; he is a bird of bad moral Character; like those among Men who live by sharping and robbing, he is generally poor, and often very lousy. The Turkey is a much more respectable Bird and withal a true, original native of America."

2. AN OLIVE BRANCH: The olive branch symbolizes peace. Long ago, the eagle looked toward the talon with the arrows. President Harry Truman had the head turned in the direction of the olive branch so that the seal would stand for peace.

3. THIRTEEN: This is the number of states originally in the Union.

4. FROM MANY, ONE: This motto is pronounced "ee ploor i bus yoo nem." It stands for the unity of the country. The phrase appears on United States coins.

The Great Seal of the United States appears on the back of every dollar. The pyramid is a symbol of strength. It is unfinished, to suggest that the work of building a great nation never ends. The eye stands for providence (God) looking after the nation. The phrase "Annuit Coeptis" means "He has favored our undertaking." "Novus Ordo Seclorum" means "A new order of the ages."

5. FIFTY: The circle of stars contains one star for each state.

6. A SHIELD: The red and white stripes represent both the United States flag and the unity of the thirteen original states. The shield's top part (blue) stands for Congress. William Barton, who helped design the Great Seal in 1782, said that the color white is for purity, red for valor, and blue for vigilence and justice.

KNOW YOUR HEROES

One way to become a leader is to find heroes who will serve as models. They could be people in your life: a family member, a teacher, or a neighbor. They may be from the past, for example, Mexican leader Benito Juarez or scientist Marie Curie. They could be from stories, for example, Charlotte (the spider) or Superman.

Try this: *Use the chart below to help find your heroes. Choose your favorite hero and tell why that person is number one.*

Two Presidents' Heroes

Woodrow Wilson admired William Gladstone. Gladstone was a 19th-century British leader who served four times as prime minister. He was famous as a great orator and for his high moral values. Wilson told his father: "This Gladstone is the greatest statesman who ever lived. I intend to be a great statesman too."

Dwight Eisenhower admired Hannibal. Hannibal was a military genius born in Carthage (North Africa) in 247 B.C. During the Second Punic War, he invaded Italy by crossing the Alps. His supplies were carried by a herd of elephants. At Cannae, he won one of the most famous battles in history. A book entitled *The Life of Hannibal* made Eisenhower want to become a soldier.

QUALITY	HERO WITH THIS QUALITY
Confidence	_____
Courage	_____
Creativity	_____
Intelligence	_____
Strength	_____

Bonus: *Tell the world about your hero. You might do this by writing an article for your school paper. Or, if you like to draw, try creating a picture book, which you could then read to children younger than you. You might even offer a copy to your school or local library.*

SPEAK UP

When Harry Truman was running for President, he gave more than 300 speeches in one month. His record was 16 in one day!

But the President doesn't stop making speeches after the election. In office, you'll speak to Congress about laws you want passed. At the United Nations, you'll discuss world problems. On trips, you'll speak to people in other lands. At home, you'll make televised speeches to share your ideas with the American people.

Try this: *Write and deliver your own presidential speech. It could be for a campaign or it could be about any topic that interests the American people.*

The Value of Writing Your Own Speeches

These days, Presidents hire speech writers. But in the past, most leaders wrote their own speeches. In one case, this may have saved a President's life.

Teddy Roosevelt was in Milwaukee to deliver a speech. He wrote the words in large letters to make them easier to read. The speech filled 50 pages.

President Roosevelt folded the pages in half and placed them in his left breast pocket. On his way to the auditorium, he was shot in the chest by John Shrank. Roosevelt was rushed to the hospital. Doctors found that the thick pages had slowed the bullet, thus preventing serious injury or even death.

President Roosevelt was able to leave the hospital and give his speech.

Tips for Public Speaking

1. Rehearse the speech several times. Give extra attention to the first few lines so that you won't begin with an "um."

2. Make a smooth entrance. Get set before you say anything. If you like, smile at the audience.

3. Speak clearly and loud enough to be heard at the back of the room. Don't rush your words.

4. Make eye contact. If you are reading your speech, look at the audience from time to time.

5. Have a strong ending. Don't fidget or say something weak like, "Well, I guess that's it." You might thank the audience for their attention. Then leave the stage.

6. Evaluate your speech. Give yourself credit for what you did well. How can you do better next time?

Bonus: *To get ready for a radio speech, record yourself on tape. If you know someone with a camcorder, practice for TV by reading a speech while facing the lens.*

IMPROVE YOUR MEMORY

As President, you will be meeting hundreds of strangers each year. If you can remember their names and what they do, you will make them feel good.

Try this: *Practice remembering. Study each picture and caption below. Then, look at the Memory Test and see if you can remember each person's name and job.*

Ben Franklin,
statesman, inventor

Harriet Tubman,
freedom fighter

Robert E. Lee,
general

Albert Einstein,
mathematician

Amelia Earhart,
pilot

Mark Twain,
author

Pablo Picasso,
painter

Chief Joseph,
Nez Perce leader

Sandra Day O'Connor,
Supreme Court justice

MEMORY TEST

Name each person and tell why the person is famous. The answers are on the Improve Your Memory page.

BE A PROBLEM SOLVER

Murphy's law says: "Anything that can go wrong, will go wrong." Trouble usually comes along at the worst possible time: Shoelaces break when you're in a hurry. The book you need for a report is missing.

As President, things won't get any easier. In fact, you'll face some of the world's biggest problems.

Bonus: *Pick one of the big problems now facing our country. Learn all you can about it. Then send a letter about your plan to solve it to someone who is supposed to deal with that kind of problem, for example, the governor, the mayor, or the President.*

Try this: *You can prepare to be a problem-solving leader by studying problems that you have already faced. Make a list of problems from your past, for example, getting lost on a camping trip or being late for an important event. Describe what you did to solve the problem.*

Problem-Solving Tips

1. Make sure you know what the problem is. Try stating it in a single sentence. Include a goal, for example, "I want to be able to . . . "

2. Look for a solution. See if you can think of a similar problem that you or someone else solved in the past. If possible, invite other people to help you dream up a solution.

3. List the resources your solution calls for. Make sure they're available. For example, if you were lost, you might want a map. But if a map isn't available, "Reading a map" would not be a good solution.

4. List the steps you would follow to solve the problem. Be as detailed as possible.

5. Carry out the steps. If things don't work out the way you hoped, try to figure out what changes might improve your plan.

KNOW THE WORLD

Most of the federal government's offices are in the capital, Washington, D.C. That's why Presidents spend so much time there.

But these days, what happens around the world affects life in the United States. For this reason, Presidents must often travel all over the world. Their trips deal with such issues as trade, war and peace, and the environment.

Try this: *On the world map (see resource page) write each President's name next to the country he was the first to visit while in office.*

PLACE	FIRST VISITED BY
Canada	Harding
China	Nixon
Egypt	F. Roosevelt
France	Wilson
Iran	F. Roosevelt
Italy	F. Roosevelt
Japan	Reagan
Mexico	Taft
Morocco	F. Roosevelt
Panama	T. Roosevelt
Russia	Nixon
Saudi Arabia	Bush

Geographical Facts Every President Should Know

You should be able to name the following places and/or locate them on a map:

- The seven continents
- The five largest oceans
- The world's five longest rivers
- The countries of North America, Central America, and South America
- The countries of Africa
- The countries of Europe
- The countries of the Middle East
- The countries of Asia
- The world's 10 largest cities
- The capitals of the 10 largest countries
- The equator
- The Tropic of Cancer
- The Tropic of Capricorn
- The international date line

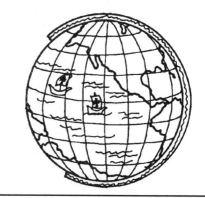

Bonus: *Write about the country you most want to visit. Tell why you want to go there.*

★WORLD MAP★

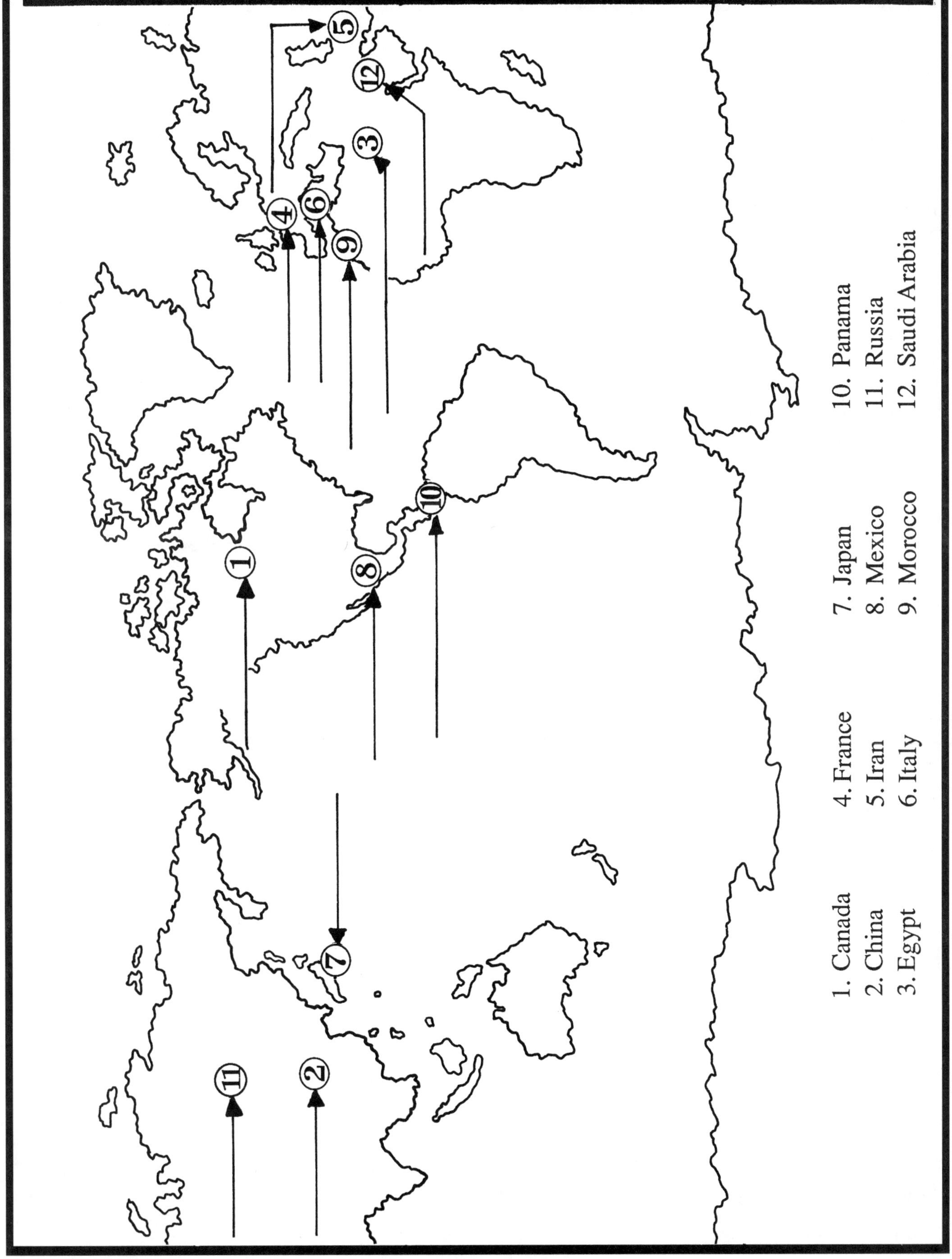

1. Canada
2. China
3. Egypt

4. France
5. Iran
6. Italy

7. Japan
8. Mexico
9. Morocco

10. Panama
11. Russia
12. Saudi Arabia

PRACTICE YOUR SIGNATURE

As President, your signature has great importance. For example, when Congress sends you a bill (a proposed law), it becomes a real law when you sign it. You will also sign important proclamations (announcements). One of the most famous examples is Lincoln's proclamation that freed the slaves in the Confederate states.

Finally, you will sign treaties. These agreements between countries cover many subjects, such as trade, pollution, boundaries, and fishing rights.

Try this: *Because you will be signing so many important papers, you should practice your signature. Begin by studying the presidential signatures shown here. In the box below, sign your name five or six times. Choose the one you like best.*

Sample Signatures

George Washington

Abraham Lincoln

Your Signature

Bonus: *Handwriting experts claim they can tell a lot about people by studying their handwriting. What do you think? Read a book about handwriting. Then study your own handwriting.*

PART 3

GET ELECTED

The ballot is stronger than the bullet.
Abraham Lincoln
May 19, 1856

WRITE YOUR STORY

When you run for President, the voters will want to know all about you. Reporters will, too. You will be able to answer their questions by writing a short autobiography (the story of your life) ahead of time.

Try this: *Write your story. Start by filling out the fact sheet below. You might include other facts on topics not covered here. Use this information when you write your autobiography. You might include a photo or drawing of yourself.*

AUTOBIOGRAPHY FACT SHEET

Birth date: _____ Birthplace: _____

Ancestry (for example, Dutch, African, French): _____

_____

Parents' names: _____

Grandparents' names: _____

Others in your family: _____

_____

Best school subject: _____

Work experience (include household chores): _____

_____

Clubs: _____

Heroes: _____

Achievements and important experiences (e.g., trips): _____

_____

Goals: _____

Bonus: *Read a biography of one of your favorite Presidents.*

★LINCOLN'S AUTOBIOGRAPHY★

(Written in June 1860, for the presidential campaign)

I was born February 12, 1809, in Hardin County, Kentucky. My parents were both born in Virginia, of undistinguished families — second families, perhaps I should say. My mother, who died in my tenth year, was of a family of the name of Hanks, some of whom now reside in Adams, and others in Macon County, Illinois. My paternal grandfather, Abraham Lincoln, emigrated from Rockingham County, Virginia, to Kentucky about 1781 or 1782, where a year or two later he was killed by the Indians, not in battle but by stealth, when he was laboring to open a farm in the forest . . .

My father, at the death of his father, was but six years of age, and he grew up literally without education. He removed from Kentucky to what is now Spencer County, Indiana, in my eighth year. We reached our new home about the time the State came into the Union. It was a wild region, with many bears and other wild animals still in the woods. There I grew up. There were some schools, so called, but no qualification was ever required of a teacher beyond "readin', writin', and cipherin' " to the rule of three. If a straggler supposed to understand Latin happened to sojourn in the neighborhood, he was looked upon as a wizard. There was absolutely nothing to excite ambition for education. Of course, when I came of age I did not know much. Still, somehow, I could read, write, and cipher to the rule of three, but that was all. I have not been to school since. The little advance I now have upon this store of education, I have picked up from time to time under the pressure of necessity.

I was raised to farm work, which I continued till I was twenty-two. At twenty-one I came to Illinois, Macon County. Then I got to New Salem, at that time in Sangamon, now in Menard County, where I remained a year as a sort of clerk in a store. Then came the Black Hawk War; and I was elected a captain of volunteers, a success which gave me more pleasure than any I have had since. I went [to] the campaign, was elected, ran for the Legislature the same year (1832) and was beaten. The next and three succeeding biennial elections I was elected to the Legislature. I was not a candidate afterward. During this legislative period I had studied law and removed to Springfield to practice it. In 1846 I was once elected to the Lower House of Congress . . .

If any personal description of me is thought desirable, it may be said that I am, in height, six feet four inches, nearly; lean in flesh, weighing on an average one hundred and eighty pounds; dark complexion, with coarse black hair and gray eyes. No other marks or brands recollected.

TELL WHY YOU'RE RUNNING

When you decide to run for President, people will ask you why. After all, it is one of the most difficult jobs in the world. It's also dangerous. Ten Presidents have been shot at and four have been killed.

Try this: *Check the reasons you would like to be President. Add other reasons that come to mind.*

☐ Become famous

☐ Earn a place in history

☐ Fly in Air Force One

☐ Live in a mansion

☐ Get to invite movie stars and other celebrities to dinner

☐ Solve the United States' problems

☐ Solve the world's problems

☐ Travel to interesting places

☐ _____

☐ _____

☐ _____

What Presidents Have Said About Being President

"I know that when things don't go well they like to blame the Presidents, and that's one of the things which Presidents are paid for."
—John F. Kennedy

"It brings nothing but increasing drudgery and daily loss of friends."
—Thomas Jefferson

"If you are as happy, my dear sir, on entering this house (the White House) as I am in leaving it and returning home, you are the happiest man in this country."
—James Buchanan to Abe Lincoln

"The President is at liberty both in law and in conscience to be as big a man as he can."
—Woodrow Wilson

"I would rather have peace in the world than be President."
—Harry Truman

Bonus: *Ask a local leader, such as your mayor, his or her reasons for seeking the job.*

TAKE A STAND

Great leaders have strong beliefs. They're also willing to state them honestly and clearly.

Try this: *Decide where you stand on the following issues. Check whether you agree or disagree with each statement.*

	I AGREE	I DISAGREE
1. Animals should have the same rights as people.	☐	☐
2. Elementary school children should be allowed to vote.	☐	☐
3. People should be required to eat healthy diets.	☐	☐
4. Everyone should have to dress neatly.	☐	☐
5. Violent movies should be outlawed.	☐	☐
6. The U.S. should send money to countries that are poor.	☐	☐
7. TV viewing should be limited to a certain number of hours a day.	☐	☐

Animals Have Rights, Too!

Bonus: *Presidents must also give their reasons for their opinions. Practice this skill by writing a paragraph about one or more of the opinions you just gave. You might also read newspapers and watch TV to see what other leaders think about these topics.*

COMPARE YOURSELF

While all Presidents to date have been white males, they weren't all alike. Some were rich; others were poor. Some were world travelers; others stayed near home. Many were tall (Abe Lincoln was 6' 4"), while others were short (James Madison was 5' 4").

Try this: *In the chart below, list facts about yourself. Then look at Presidential Facts (resource page) to learn how you are like Presidents who came before you. Also, pay attention to the differences.*

FACTS ABOUT ME

Grade now in: _____ Goal (high school, college): _____

Favorite book: _____

Favorite dessert: _____

Favorite food: _____

Favorite song: _____

Hair color: _____

Hobbies: _____

Type of building born in (hospital, log cabin): _____

Musical instruments played: _____

Nickname: _____

Pets: _____

Favorite sports and games: _____

Bonus: *Pick one of the facts about yourself and explain why it could help you be a good President.*

★PRESIDENTIAL FACTS★

EDUCATION
Attended graduate school: Wilson
Attended Military Academy: Grant
Didn't attend college: Washington
Never went to school: A. Johnson

FAVORITE BOOK
The Arabian Nights: J.Q. Adams
Ivanhoe: Grant
James Bond series: Kennedy
Wind in the Willows: T. Roosevelt

FAVORITE DESSERT
Apple pie: F. Roosevelt
Apples, fried: Grant
Blackberry jam: Jackson
Chocolate anything: Kennedy
Prune whip: Eisenhower

FAVORITE FOOD
Canned green peas: L. Johnson
Cucumbers soaked in vinegar: Grant
Fettucini: Kennedy
Frogs' legs: F. Roosevelt
Grapefruit juice and raw eggs: Wilson
Knockwurst and sauerkraut: Harding

FAVORITE SONG
"Amazing Grace": Carter
"Home on the Range": Nixon
"Oklahoma": Ford
"Twenty Years Ago": Lincoln

HAIR COLOR
Black: 3
Blond: 2
Brown: 22
Red: 3
Reddish brown: 2

HOBBY
Diary writing: J.Q. Adams
Flying roosters: Van Buren
Juggling: Garfield
Riding an electric horse: Coolidge
Stamp collecting: F. Roosevelt

HOUSING BORN IN
Log cabin: Lincoln
Mansion: Washington

MUSICAL INSTRUMENT
Piano: Truman
Trombone: Harding

NICKNAME
J. Adams: Old Sink or Swim
Ford: Mr. Nice Guy
Lincoln: Honest Abe
Roosevelt: Four Eyes
Taft: Smiling Bill
Washington: Old Muttonhead

PET

Bear: T. Roosevelt
Bird: T. Roosevelt
Cat: Lincoln
Cow: Taft
Dog: Bush
Donkey: Coolidge
Pony: T. Roosevelt

SPORTS AND GAMES
Boxing: Buchanan
Fishing: Carter
Football: Ford
Golf: Eisenhower
Jogging: Bush

MAKE A MOTTO

In a few words, a campaign motto tells something important about a candidate. It might say:

- What the person believes in
- What the person promises to do
- What makes the person special

Presidential candidates often use mottoes in speeches and on posters.

Try this: *Write your campaign motto. Begin by listing topics that matter to you, for example, freedom, honesty, or hunger. Create several mottoes about each topic. Then pick the one you like best. Print your motto on a button, bumper sticker, banner, or poster. You might add a picture to help get your idea across.*

Campaign Mottoes

"Keep the ball rolling."
    William H. Harrison, 1841

"Don't swap horses."
    Abraham Lincoln, 1864

"We love him for the enemies he has made."
    Grover Cleveland, 1885

"He kept us out of war."
    Woodrow Wilson, 1916

Bonus: *If your town or school doesn't have a motto, create one yourself. Or work with people to hold a motto-writing contest.*

Story of the U. S. Motto

On September 13, 1814, British ships fired on Fort McHenry, near Baltimore. When the attack ended 25 hours later, the United States flag was still flying.

Francis Scott Key watched the battle. His poem about it was set to music and became the national anthem. It contains the lines:

Then Conquer we must,
When our cause it is just
And this be our motto:
"In God is our trust."

During the Civil War, a minister named M.R. Watkinson wrote to the U.S. Secretary of the Treasury:

"From my heart I have felt our national shame in disowning God." The minister suggested that God be mentioned on the country's coins.

The Secretary liked the idea and used Francis Key's phrase with a slight change: "In God we trust."

Those words began to appear on coins in 1864. In 1955, Congress ordered the motto placed on all money. The next year, it became the national motto.

WRITE A CAMPAIGN SONG

When you campaign for office, you want to excite and inspire the people who might vote for you. Many candidates have done this by creating a campaign song. They often borrow an old tune and write new words.

Try this: *Use the following steps to create your own campaign tune.*

Ronald Reagan's Campaign Song, 1976
(to the tune of "The Battle Hymn of the Republic")

He has braved the troubled waters,
He has flown across the skies,
He's the man from California,
He's the one we idolize,
He is headed for the White House
He will never compromise,
He will win in '76.
Ronnie, Ronnie, Ronnie Reagan,
Ronnie, Ronnie, Ronnie Reagan,
Ronnie, Ronnie, Ronnie Reagan,
He'll win in '76.

Step 1. List a few points that you want to cover in your song. These might have to do with your talents or goals.

Step 2. Choose a melody. It should have a rhythm that you can easily set words to, and its mood should probably be upbeat. Some melodies that might work are "Twinkle, Twinkle, Little Star," "For He's a Jolly Good Fellow," and "Yankee Doodle."

Step 3. Write the words. As you work, keep the tune in mind by humming it or playing it on a musical instrument. Try to come up with easy-to-remember rhymes.

Step 4. Rewrite if necessary. You may need to make many changes to get the rhythm and the rhymes correct. Check the words by singing them to the music.

Step 5. Test the song. Ask a few friends to try it. Are the words easy to remember and fun to sing?

FIND OUT ABOUT PARTIES

The Constitution does not mention political parties. But you must learn about them if you want to be President.

A political party is a group of voters. They share ideas about the goals of government. One party might be interested in helping businesses grow. Another party might focus on the environment.

All parties nominate (pick) people to run for office. Each candidate promises to support the party's ideas.

There are many political parties. But for decades, every President has belonged to either the Democratic or the Republican party.

Try this: *Write to different parties. Ask for literature that tells what they stand for. You'll find addresses of minor parties in almanacs under "Political parties." The addresses of the two major parties are:*

Democratic Party
430 S. Capitol St., SE
Washington, DC 20003

Republican Party
310 First St., SE
Washington, DC 20003

Bonus: *Interview voters from different parties. Ask what they believe about such issues as crime, education, the environment, and welfare. Try to learn how parties are alike and different.*

Examples of Minor Parties and What They Stood For

Anti-Masonic (1832): Against secret clubs
Liberty (1844): Anti-slavery
Free Soil (1848): Anti-slavery
Know Nothing (1856): Anti-immigration
Greenback (1876): Pro-labor
Prohibition (1884): Anti-liquor
Woman Suffrage (1888): Women's right to vote
Populist (1892): End national banks
Socialist (1900-1920): For public ownership of certain industries
Bull Moose (1912): For free trade
Progressive (1924): Pro-farmer, pro-labor
States Rights (1948): Less federal power
American (1972): Pro-law and order

KNOW CAMPAIGN TALK

Every activity has its own special words. For example, when playing football you'll hear words like "punt," "tackle," and "quarterback." If you're an astronomer, you'll know about "telescope" and "satellite."

It's the same when you campaign for office. You've got to be able to speak and understand political talk.

Try this: *Read newspapers from a campaign year. When you see one of the words or phrases below, check it off.*

☐ "Caucus": A private meeting where a group of voters picks a candidate or decides on a plan.

☐ "Climbing on the bandwagon": Supporting a candidate just because others are doing so.

☐ "Convention": A meeting where a political party picks candidates for President and Vice President.

☐ "Dark horse": A candidate who has little chance to win.

☐ "Delegation": A group at a convention; they represent party members of their state or district.

☐ "Favorite son" or "Favorite daughter": A candidate who is supported by people from his or her own state.

☐ "Front runner": Someone who is favored to win an election.

☐ "Keynote address": A speech given at the start of a convention.

☐ "Media": TV, newspapers, and other ways of sharing news.

☐ "Nominee": A party's choice to run for office.

☐ "Plank": A belief held by a party. For example, "Public schools must get more money."

☐ "Platform": All the major beliefs (planks) of a party.

☐ "Poll": A sample election done to learn how people might vote.

☐ "Primary": An election to choose a party's candidate.

☐ "Registered voter": Someone who has signed up to vote.

☐ "Ticket": A party's candidates for President and Vice President.

COUNT THE RETURNS

Every four years, a presidential election takes place on the first Tuesday after the first Monday in November.

Voters don't actually vote for the candidates. Instead, they vote for "electors" who promise to choose one candidate or another in a second election. (Many people don't like this two-step system. But to change it means changing the Constitution, and that is never an easy job.)

Each state has as many electors as it has members in Congress. A state with a big population like Texas has about 30 electors. A smaller state like North Dakota has three.

Try this: *Use the Voting Score Sheet (below) to sum up the results of a past or current election. List each candidate's popular votes (votes cast by the people) and electoral votes.*

Note: The candidate who gets the most "popular" votes in a state (or territory) wins all the electoral votes in that place. Suppose one candidate gets 50,000 popular votes, and the other candidate gets one vote less (49,999). Then the first candidate wins all of the electoral votes.

There are currently 538 electors throughout the United States. To win the presidency, you need 270 electoral votes.

VOTING SCORE SHEET

Candidate	Popular Vote	Electoral Vote
_____	_____	_____
_____	_____	_____
_____	_____	_____
_____	_____	_____

Bonus: *Follow a past or current election. Assign each party a color. On the Electoral Map (see resource page), color in the states that each candidate wins. Is there a geographical pattern? For example, did one candidate win most or all of the coastal states or the Northern states?*

★ELECTORAL MAP★

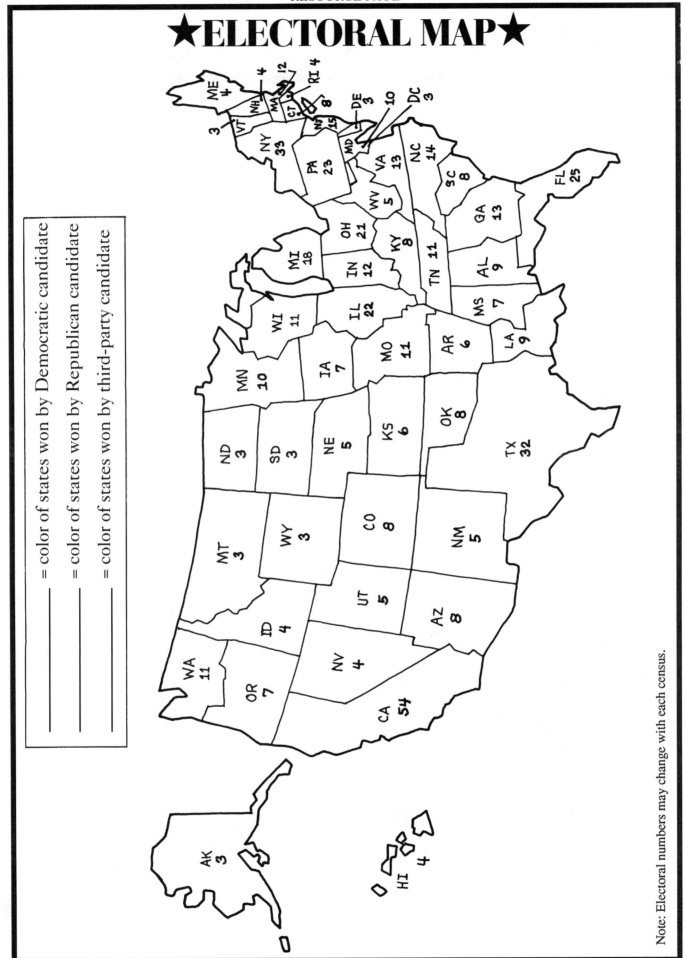

= color of states won by Democratic candidate

= color of states won by Republican candidate

= color of states won by third-party candidate

ME 4

NH 4

VT 3

MA 12

RI 4

CT 8

NY 33

NJ 15

PA 23

DE 3

MD 10

DC 3

WV 5

VA 13

NC 14

SC 8

FL 25

GA 13

OH 21

KY 8

TN 11

AL 9

MI 18

IN 12

MS 7

IL 22

LA 9

WI 11

MO 11

AR 6

MN 10

IA 7

OK 8

TX 32

ND 3

SD 3

NE 5

KS 6

MT 3

WY 3

CO 8

NM 5

UT 5

AZ 8

ID 4

NV 4

WA 11

OR 7

CA 54

AK 3

HI 4

Note: Electoral numbers may change with each census.

DON'T FEAR FAILURE

You may think of Presidents as people who are winners. After all, to be elected President of the United States means winning one of the biggest political prizes in the world.

In fact, most Presidents lost one or more elections before winning the White House. The list of losers includes Franklin Roosevelt, John Kennedy, Richard Nixon, Ronald Reagan, and George Bush. These people became winners in the long run because they learned from their defeats, and they never quit.

Try this: *Choose a disappointment that you had at school, in sports, or in a project (play, recital). Write about the lesson you learned from the experience. Describe what happened and how it helped you to become a more successful person.*

Lincoln's Losses

Before winning the presidency in 1860, Abe Lincoln won several posts, but he also suffered many disappointments:

1831 Failed in business

1832 Defeated in a bid for the Illinois General Assembly

1834 Failed in business

1838 Defeated in a bid for speaker of the Illinois House of Representatives

1840 Defeated in a bid for becoming a Whig party elector

1843 Defeated in a bid for the U.S. House of Representatives

1855 Defeated in a bid for the U.S. Senate

1856 Defeated in a bid for the Republican vice-presidential nomination

1858 Defeated in a bid for the U.S. Senate

Bonus: *Learn about a person who faced many disappointments. It could be someone famous, for example, Elizabeth Cady Stanton, who battled for women's rights. Or it could be a neighbor or a member of your family.*

PART 4

TAKE OFFICE

This great nation will endure as it has endured, will revive and will prosper. So, first of all, let me assert my firm belief that the only thing we have to fear is fear itself.
Franklin Roosevelt
Inaugural Address
March 4, 1933

PLAN YOUR INAUGURATION

If you win the November election, you'll become President on January 20 by reciting an oath: "I do solemnly swear (or affirm) that I will faithfully execute the Office of President of the United States, and will to the best of my ability, preserve, protect and defend the Constitution of the United States."

In good weather, you'll do this on the Capitol steps. You'll then give an inaugural address and listen to bands play the President's song: "Hail to the Chief." Later, in ballrooms throughout Washington, people will dance, eat, and enjoy performances by top entertainers.

Try this: *Write your inaugural address. You might wish to cover:*
- *Problems the nation must solve*
- *Changes you'd like to make*
- *Advice for your fellow Americans*

Bonus: *Plan your inaugural ball. Decide on the following: the band, the food, and famous entertainers.*

Inaugural Address

BY JOHN KENNEDY (JANUARY 20, 1961)

Let the word go forth from this time and place, to friend and foe alike, that the torch has been passed to a new generation of Americans, born in this century, tempered by war, disciplined by a hard and bitter peace, proud of our ancient heritage, and unwilling to witness or permit the slow undoing of those human rights to which this nation has always been committed . . .

Let every nation know, whether it wishes us well or ill, that we shall pay any price, bear any burden, meet any hardship, support any friend, oppose any foe to assure the survival and the success of liberty.

. . . If a free society cannot help the many who are poor, it cannot save the few who are rich.

. . . All this will not be finished in the first one hundred days. Nor will it be finished in the first one thousand days, nor in the life of this Administration, nor even perhaps in our lifetime on this planet. But let us begin.

. . . Now the trumpet summons us again—not as a call to bear arms, though arms we need . . . not as a call to battle, though embattled we are—but as a call to bear the burden of a long twilight struggle, year in and year out, "rejoicing in hope, patient in tribulation," a struggle against the common enemies of man: tyranny, poverty, disease and war itself . . .

And so, my fellow Americans, ask not what your country can do for you; ask what you can do for your country.

KNOW THE WHITE HOUSE

The White House won't just be your home when you're President. You'll use it as your office and as a place to entertain guests. The White House is also a museum visited by Americans and people from around the globe.

Try this: *Get to know your new home. Take the following quiz about one of the world's most famous buildings.*

WHITE HOUSE QUIZ

1. When it was built, the White House was
    A. red   B. white   C. blue   D. gray

2. The land on which the White House stands is
    A. 1 acre   B. 9 acres   C. 18 acres

3. The White House is made of
    A. wood   B. sandstone   C. brick

4. At different times during its history, the White House was called
    A. The President's Palace
    B. Washington Monument
    C. The Lincoln Monument

5. Each year, the White House is visited by about
    A. 1,000 tourists   B. 100,000 tourists   C. 1,000,000 tourists

6. Visitors may visit the President's bedroom
    A. only in the day   B. only at night   C. never

7. In 1814, the original White House was burned down by
    A. lightning   B. British soldiers   C. a careless smoker

8. At the White House you can find
    A. a bowling alley B. a swimming pool C. a movie theater D. all three

9. The President's office is located
    A. in the basement   B. in the West Wing   C. on the roof

10. The shape of the President's office is
    A. square   B. triangular   C. oval

1.D, 2.C, 3.B, 4.A, 5.C, 6.C, 7.B, 8.D, 9.B, 10.C

Answers

★THE WHITE HOUSE★

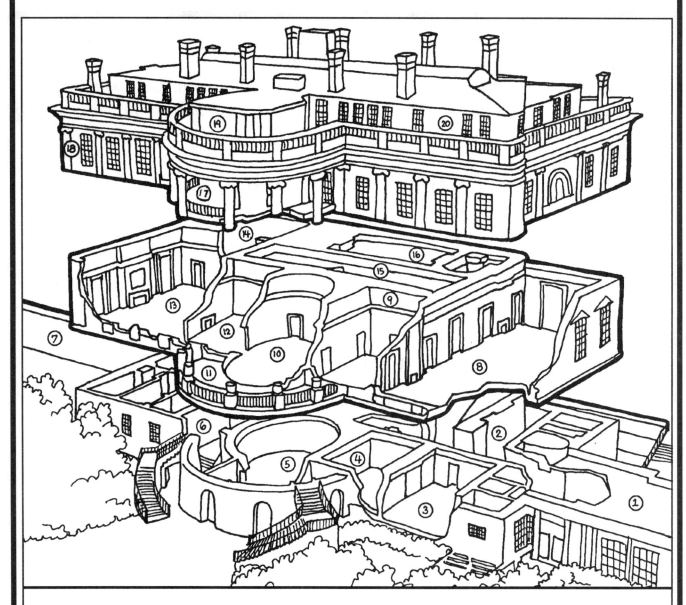

1. East Wing Corridor: includes movie theater for the first family
2. Library: contains 2,700 books on American life
3. Vermeil Room: displays silver for state dinners
4. China Room: displays china for state dinners
5. Diplomatic Reception Room: formal entrance
6. Map Room
7. West Wing Corridor: leads to the Oval Office where the President works and meets with aides
8. East Room: largest of the White House's 132 rooms; used for parties, press conferences, ballets, concerts, and weddings
9. Green Room: a parlor (sitting room) with green silk wall covering
10. Blue Room: where the President meets visitors
11. South Portico: a covered porch
12. Red Room: a parlor with red silk wall covering
13. State Dining Room: seats 140 for lunch or dinner
14. Family Dining Room
15. Cross Hall: connects State Dining Room and East Room
16. Entrance Hall
17. Truman Balcony
18. Family Living Quarters
19. Solarium: glassed-in sun room where John Kennedy's children had school
20. Staff Living Quarters

GET TO KNOW WASHINGTON

Washington, D.C., isn't part of any state. "D.C." stands for "District of Columbia," land given by Maryland and Virginia. George Washington chose the place in 1790 for the new capital, designed by Pierre L'Enfant.

As President, you may show visitors Washington's famous monuments, museums, and other attractions. Luckily, the capital is a small, easy-to-know town, just 63 square miles. (By comparison, Kansas City is 316 square miles, and Paris is 432 square miles.)

Try this: *Tour Washington. Use the D.C. Walking Tour (see resource page). Trace your journey on the Washington Map (below) with a marker or pencil.*

You'll find that many of the landmarks are within walking distance of the White House. But if you get tired, hop on a jitney or the Metro (subway).

Bonus: *Create a guide to places in your town for tourists to use after you gain fame as President.*

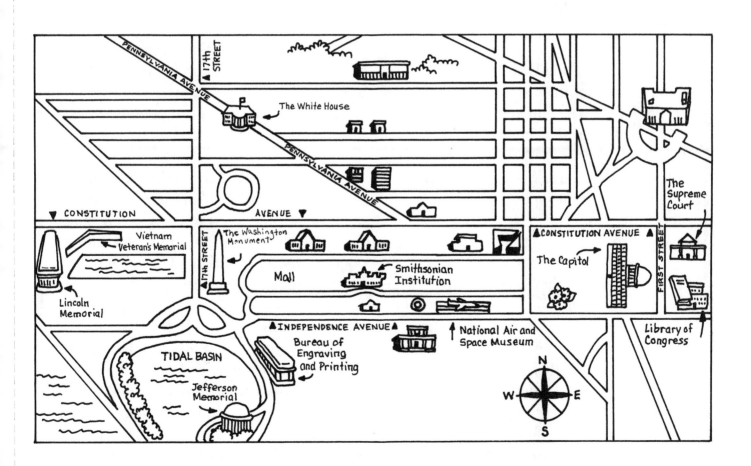

★D.C. WALKING TOUR★

From the 1) WHITE HOUSE, walk south on 17th Street to the . . .

2) WASHINGTON MONUMENT. Take the 555-foot, minute-long elevator ride to the top of the world's tallest marble structure (built 1848-1884). Enjoy the city's best views: east to the Capitol (where Congress meets), north to the White House, south to the Jefferson Memorial, and west to the Lincoln Memorial. Saturdays, you can walk down the 897 steps, if you're hardy. Head west. On the right is the . . .

3) VIETNAM VETERANS MEMORIAL. This 300-foot-long set of black granite tablets names the 57,213 United States soldiers killed in Vietnam. Walk southwest to the . . .

4) LINCOLN MEMORIAL. The 36 columns represent the states of the Union in 1865. Lincoln's giant statue faces the 2,000-foot-long reflecting pool. Here, in 1963, 200,000 people heard Martin Luther King, Jr., give his famous "I have a dream" civil rights speech. Go south around the Tidal Basin (where cherry trees bloom each spring) to the . . .

5) JEFFERSON MEMORIAL, honoring the author of the Declaration of Independence. Head northeast to the . . .

6) BUREAU OF ENGRAVING AND PRINTING, where the United States prints all its bonds, postage stamps, and paper money ($25.5 million daily). Don't expect free samples. Go northeast to the . . .

7) MALL, a park between the Washington Monument and the Capitol, and surrounded by nine of the country's best museums. Look for a red-brick building, the first home of the . . .

8) SMITHSONIAN INSTITUTION. This vast museum and research center was a gift of British scientist James Smithson, who never even visited the United States. Continue east to the . . .

9) NATIONAL AIR AND SPACE MUSEUM. The most popular museum in the world houses the plane that the Wright brothers flew at Kitty Hawk, Lindbergh's "Spirit of St. Louis," and the X-1 rocket plane that broke the sound barrier. Go east on Independence to the . . .

10) CAPITOL. This is the geographic center of town. Here, on Capitol Hill, Senators and Representatives debate new laws. Go east on Independence to First Street where you'll find the . . .

11) LIBRARY OF CONGRESS, one of the world's largest libraries. It holds most book published in the United States as well as millions of photographs, movies, documents, and artifacts. Go north on First Street to Constitution and the . . .

12) SUPREME COURT. From October to June, nine justices decide such history-making cases as *Brown v. The Board of Education of Topeka* (1954), which ended state-supported racial segregation in public schools. Go west on Constitution to 17th Street. Turn right. Walk six blocks and you're home.

PART 5

GO TO WORK

I believe that this nation should commit itself to achieving the goal, before this decade is out, of landing a man on the moon and returning him safely to the earth . . . But in a very real sense, it will not be one man going to the moon . . . it will be an entire nation, for all of us must work to put him there.
John F. Kennedy
Address to Congress
May 25, 1961

DREAM BIG

A President must know how to solve problems. But the job doesn't stop there. A leader should also have big dreams, and be able to help people make them come true.

A perfect example is John Kennedy's dream of having the United States be the first country to have astronauts visit the moon. President Kennedy spoke about this goal in a way that gained the support of millions of Americans.

Try this: *Describe three dreams you have for yourself. Think about your plans for education, family, travel, talents, and career. Tell why each dream is important to you.*

Presidential Dreams

Thomas Jefferson dreamed of doubling the size of the United States by buying millions of acres from France. The result was called the Louisiana Purchase.

Theodore Roosevelt said there should be a shorter route for ships sailing between the Atlantic and Pacific oceans. His dream became the Panama Canal.

Franklin Roosevelt wanted to make sure that senior citizens would have enough money to live on. He then helped create a program called Social Security.

Jimmy Carter dreamed of ending the conflict in the Middle East. With his help, Israel and Egypt agreed on a peace plan known as The Camp David Accords.

Someday I'll _____

_____

_____

Someday I'll _____

_____

_____

Someday I'll _____

_____

_____

Bonus: *Write about a dream you have for America. Explain why your dream would make this a better country.*

HELP MAKE LAWS

According to the Constitution, Congress makes the country's laws. The President sees that the laws are obeyed.

However, most Presidents have their own ideas about what kinds of laws are needed. In fact, Presidents often suggest laws to Congress.

Try this: *Look for problems that might be solved by new laws. Use the checklist below. Add your own ideas.*

Choose one problem. Write a letter about it to your Senator, Representative, or local newspaper. Explain why you think a new law is needed.

TOPICS THAT LAWS MIGHT DEAL WITH

☐   Air pollution

☐   Animal rights

☐   Bicycling

☐   Billboards

☐   Education

☐   Health

☐   Housing

☐   Poverty

☐   TV commercials

☐   _____

☐   _____

Topics for Laws of the Future

✓ Brain transplants

✓ ESP (mind reading)

✓ Genetic engineering (making people, animals, or plants bigger, smaller, etc.)

✓ Invisibility

✓ Space travel

✓ Time travel

✓ Visitors from other planets

Bonus: *Write a law that might be needed in the future. For example, suppose a new kind of very smart robot is invented. Your law might answer questions about what these robots will be permitted to do. When you write your law, make the "do's" and "don'ts" clear.*

★HOW LAWS GET MADE★

Cities, counties, states, and nations all make laws. Each kind of government has its own way of creating laws. The steps here show how United States laws are made.

"They shouldn't be allowed to fly so low. I'm going to write to my senator."

1. PROBLEM: The President, a Congressperson, or a citizen notices a problem that may affect the country. This gives the person an idea for a law.

2. BILL: Someone in Congress (either in the Senate or the House of Representatives) writes up the idea as a bill (a "trial" law). In this example, we'll follow a bill that starts in the Senate.

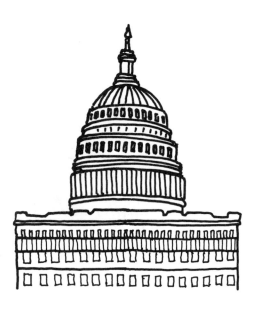

3. INTRODUCTION: The Senate clerk gives the bill a number and title. The bill then goes to a committee (a small group of lawmakers).

4. PUBLIC HEARING: The committee holds an open meeting where experts and citizens tell why they like or don't like the bill.

5. CLOSED HEARING: The committee meets privately to discuss what they learned at the public hearing. They may decide to vote against the bill. Or they may OK the bill with or without amendments (changes). If the bill is approved, it is sent to the whole Senate.

DO NOT ENTER

★HOW LAWS GET MADE★

6. DEBATE: Senators discuss questions like "Will the bill solve the problem?" and "Can the country afford it?" This talk may take only minutes. But if a bill stirs up strong feelings, debate may go on for weeks. Finally, Senators vote to approve or not approve the bill.

7. TRANSFER: If the Senate approves the bill, it is sent to the House of Representatives and goes through the same steps. The House may reject the bill, or may accept it, with or without changes.

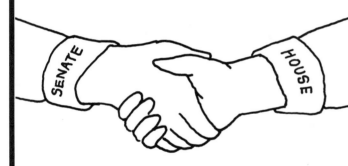

8. CONFERENCE: If the House votes for the bill with changes, a few Senators and Representatives meet as a "conference committee." They try to write a compromise bill that both branches of Congress will okay.

9. FINAL VOTE: Each branch of Congress votes on the bill. If it passes, it is signed by the top person in each branch.

10. PRESIDENTIAL APPROVAL: The bill becomes a law if the President signs it. Important laws are often signed in front of many people. If the President doesn't like the bill and refuses to sign it (vetoes it), the bill can still become law if two-thirds of the members in each branch of Congress vote for it. This is called "overriding the President's veto."

HIRE YOUR HELPERS

The federal (U.S.) government is the nation's largest employer. About three million people work in health, defense, and other jobs. Presidents manage these workers with the help of 14 department heads (bosses). They form a group of advisors called the "President's Cabinet."

Try this: *Use an almanac to learn about the Cabinet members who are now in office. Write their names in the boxes below. Note: All cabinet members are called "secretaries" except for the head of the Justice Department. That person's title is "Attorney General."*

THE CABINET

State Department (foreign relations)	**Treasury Department** (money)
Defense Department (military)	**Justice Department** (laws & courts)
Interior Department (parks)	**Agriculture Department** (farmers)
Commerce Department (business)	**Labor Department** (workers)
Health & Human Services	**Housing & Urban Development**
Transportation (travel)	**Energy** (sources of power)
Education (schools and learning)	**Veterans Affairs** (former soldiers)

Bonus: *List people who you think would make good Cabinet members. Choose from among your family, friends, neighbors, and people you know from books, movies, and TV.*

WATCH YOUR TIME

Being President will keep you busy. You may find yourself wishing there were more than 24 hours in a day. Wishing won't help. A better idea is to budget your time. Begin by watching where every hour goes.

Try this: *Use the log below to keep track of your time for a day. Tell what you did during each hour. For example, if you slept till 6:30 a.m., then showered and dressed until 7:00 a.m., on the 6:00 a.m. line write: "slept, showered, dressed."*

Log for _____
month, day, year

5:00 a.m. _____   2:00 p.m. _____

6:00 a.m. _____   3:00 p.m. _____

7:00 a.m. _____   4:00 p.m. _____

8:00 a.m. _____   5:00 p.m. _____

9:00 a.m. _____   6:00 p.m. _____

10:00 a.m. _____   7:00 p.m. _____

11:00 a.m. _____   8:00 p.m. _____

12:00 noon _____   9:00 p.m. _____

1:00 p.m. _____   10:00 p.m. _____

Bonus: *Write to a local or national leader and ask for a sample daily or weekly log. Compare your activities with that person's schedule.*

★A PRESIDENTIAL DAY★

The following fictional log is similar to real schedules that Presidents often follow.

7:00 A.M. Wake up, exercise, wash, and dress. (The first family's bedrooms, bathrooms, dining room, and other living areas are on the second floor of the White House. Tourists never come to this part of the building.)

8:00 A.M. Eat breakfast and skim several papers, such as the *Washington Post* and *The Wall Street Journal*.

9:00 A.M. Walk to the Oval Office (the President's workplace) in the West Wing of the White House. Study the day's agenda (schedule) with advisors. Read and answer a few letters. Sign documents that need your approval.

9:30 A.M. Listen to diplomatic and military advisors who brief (tell) you about important world events.

9:50 A.M. Hold a videophone (picture-telephone) conference with the prime minister of Great Britain. Discuss an upcoming visit.

10:00 A.M. Meet with a group of Congresspeople from several big cities. Talk about plans for legislation (new laws) to build low-cost housing.

10:30 A.M. Meet with Treasury Department experts to discuss a report on rising prices.

11:00 A.M. Go to the Rose Garden (outside the Oval Office) for a ceremony honoring top schoolteachers from around the country.

11:30 A.M. Discuss trade relations with a group of business leaders from South America.

NOON Meet with the head of your political party to discuss travel plans for a fund-raising trip to the West Coast.

12:30 P.M. Lunch with top advisors while preparing for an afternoon press conference. List possible questions, and prepare answers.

1:30 P.M. Meet the press.

2:30 P.M. Review your press conference with advisors. Prepare a statement about a question that you didn't answer clearly.

3:00 P.M. Watch a televised launch of a daring new space mission. Discuss it with your top science advisor.

3:30 P.M. Meet with the National Security Council to discuss the new computer security codes.

4:30 P.M. Work with a speech writer on a speech you'll deliver that evening to the National Conference of Mayors.

5:00 P.M. Sign a major new clean-air law. As TV cameras record the event, share the applause with the Congressional members who shaped the bill.

5:45 P.M. Relax with your family.

7:30 P.M. Travel to a downtown hotel where you eat dinner and deliver the speech at the Mayors' meeting.

9:30 P.M. Return home. Read reports and notes for tomorrow. Then call it a day.

MAKE A BUDGET

Most Americans work either for themselves or for companies. Some examples are barbers and farmers. This is "private enterprise" work. Government work, such as highway building, is "public sector" work and is paid for by taxes.

There's never enough tax money to pay for everything that citizens want. One important task facing a President is helping decide which work the government will do. This is called "budgeting."

Try this: *Practice your budgeting skills by making a time budget for the activities in your life: going to school, reading, talking to your family, doing chores, and so on.*

Each sliver of the pie represents one hour. If you want to spend more time playing the piano, you may have less time for playing baseball. Label each activity and give it a different color. Because you can't live without sleep, eight hours have been filled in already.

YOUR TIME BUDGET

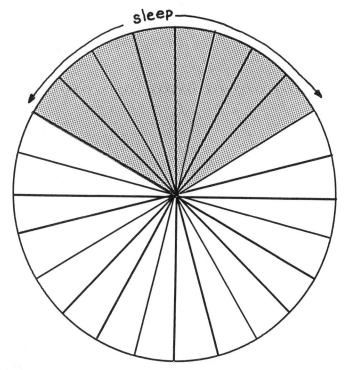

Bonus: *Take a poll. Ask each person to list the top three jobs the government should do. Make a report on what you learn.*

LEAD INTO THE FUTURE

Many Presidents have welcomed daring new ideas and inventions. For example, Franklin Roosevelt worked on a plan that brought electricity to farm areas.

Try this: *History books often tell which President was the first to do one thing or another. Check the "firsts" that you want to do as President. Add your own ideas to the list.*

	YES	NO
1. Vacation in an undersea city.	☐	☐
2. Ride the Space Shuttle.	☐	☐
3. Travel to Mars.	☐	☐
4. Meet with visitors from space.	☐	☐
5. Use ESP.	☐	☐
6. Travel in a time machine.	☐	☐
7. Hire a smart robot.	☐	☐
8. _____	☐	☐
9. _____	☐	☐

Bonus: *Talk to someone who grew up at a time when a current product (like the VCR or the telephone answering machine) didn't exist. Try to find out what life was like without that machine.*

★PRESIDENTIAL FIRSTS★

Introduced a new food to the United States (ice cream): Thomas Jefferson

Wore long pants (earlier Presidents wore knickers): James Madison

Rode on a railroad train: Andrew Jackson

Granted a news interview: Martin Van Buren

Took a bath in a White House bathtub: Millard Fillmore

Had central heating installed in the White House: Franklin Pierce

Sent and received a transatlantic telegram: James Buchanan

Was photographed in the White House: Abraham Lincoln

Used a telephone in the White House: Rutherford Hayes

Used electric lights in the White House: Benjamin Harrison (After getting a shock, he wouldn't touch the switches and would go to bed with the lights on.)

Campaigned by telephone: William McKinley

Bought first airplane for the military: Theodore Roosevelt

Talked on the radio: Warren Harding

Appeared on TV: Franklin Roosevelt

Flew in a helicopter: Dwight Eisenhower

Made a long-distance call via satellite: Lyndon Johnson

Talked to an astronaut who was on the moon: Richard Nixon

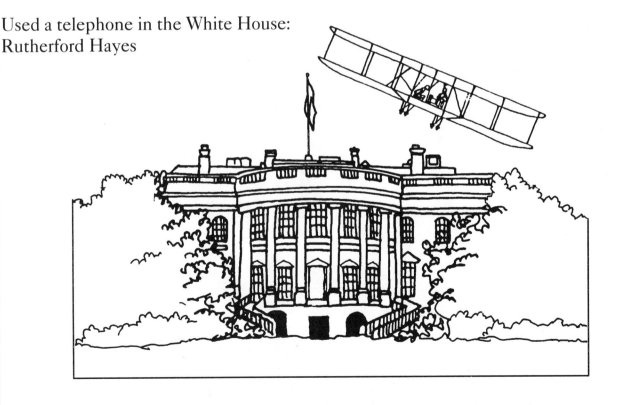

HANDLE CRISES

Most Presidents enter office with goals for making things better. They plan to build roads, improve schools, create parks, and so on.

But leaders must also deal with unexpected and sometimes terrifying problems, such as wars, earthquakes, floods, and epidemics.

Crises test a leader's courage and creativity. By successfully handling major problems, Presidents can help the nation grow stronger.

Try this: *List several big problems that you had to face, for example, getting lost or being sick. Then choose one and tell or write how you handled it and what you learned from it.*

Presidential Crises

Abraham Lincoln: On April 12, 1861, Confederate forces attacked Fort Sumter, starting the Civil War.

Herbert Hoover: In Oct. 1929, the stock market crashed. Millions of workers lost their jobs.

Franklin Roosevelt: On Dec. 7, 1941, Japanese bombers destroyed much of the U.S. Pacific Fleet in Pearl Harbor, Hawaii.

Dwight Eisenhower: On May 1, 1960, the Soviet Union shot down a U.S. "U-2" spy plane, capturing the pilot.

John F. Kennedy: In Oct. 1962, U.S. satellites discovered Soviet missiles in Cuba. The missiles could drop atomic bombs on half of the U.S. territory.

Crisis 1 _____

Crisis 2 _____

Crisis 3 _____

Crisis 4 _____

Bonus: *Choose one of the presidential crises listed on this page. Use library resources to find out how the President dealt with it. Try writing a speech that would help the American people face the crisis.*

★THE CHALLENGER DISASTER★

On January 28, 1986, the space shuttle Challenger exploded nine miles over the Atlantic. Seven astronauts were killed, including Christa McAuliffe, a New Hampshire teacher.

President Ronald Reagan met with his aides about how to help the country deal with the tragedy. Peggy Noonan, a top speech writer, went to work using notes of that meeting. A few hours later, the President gave the following speech to the nation:

Ladies and gentlemen, I had planned to speak to you tonight to report on the State of the Union, but the events of earlier today have led me to change those plans. Today is a day for mourning and remembering.

Nancy and I are pained to the core by the tragedy of the shuttle *Challenger*. We know we share this pain with all of the people of our country. This is truly a national loss . . .

We mourn seven heroes—Michael Smith, Dick Scobee, Judith Resnik, Ronald McNair, Ellison Onizuka, Gregory Jarvis, and Christa McAuliffe. We mourn their loss as a nation, together.

To the families of the seven: We cannot bear, as you do, the full impact of this tragedy—but we feel the loss, and we are thinking about you so very much. Your loved ones were daring and brave and they had that special grace, that special spirit that says, "Give me a challenge and I'll meet it with joy." They had a hunger to explore the universe and discover its truths. They wished to serve and they did—they served us all.

And I want to say something to the school children of America who were watching the live coverage of the shuttle's takeoff. I know it's hard to understand, but sometimes painful things like this happen—it's all part of the process of exploration and discovery—it's all part of taking a chance and expanding man's horizons. The future doesn't belong to the fainthearted, it belongs to the brave. The *Challenger* crew was pulling us into the future—and we'll continue to follow them.

I've always had great faith in and respect for our space program—and what happened today does nothing to diminish it. We don't hide our space program, we don't keep secrets and cover things up, we do it all up front and in public. That's the way freedom is, and we wouldn't change it for a minute.

We'll continue our quest in space. There will be more shuttle flights and more shuttle crews and, yes, more volunteers, more civilians, more teachers in space. Nothing ends here—our hopes and our journeys continue . . .

There's a coincidence today. On this day 390 years ago the great explorer Sir Francis Drake died aboard ship off the coast of Panama. In his lifetime the great frontiers were the oceans. And a historian later said, "He lived by the sea, died on it, and was buried in it." Today we can say of the *Challenger* crew: Their dedication was, like Drake's, complete.

The crew of the space shuttle *Challenger* honored us by the manner in which they lived their lives. We will never forget them, nor the last time we saw them—this morning, as they prepared for their journey, and waved good-bye, and "slipped the surly bonds of earth" to "touch the face of God."

STAY IN TOUCH

As President, you'll spend time with famous people. You'll live in a mansion (the White House) with servants. You'll have a limousine and fly in your own jet. You won't worry about traffic jams and busy airports. This life may sound nice, but it might make you forget that you work for the "ordinary" people.

Try this: *Keep in mind that if you want to improve this country, you must stay close to your fellow Americans. Read the list below. Check the ideas that make sense. Add your own. Then pick one plan and write a story showing how you would carry it out. Add details, for example, wearing a disguise to a ball game so that you won't be mobbed.*

STAYING CLOSE TO THE PEOPLE

- [ ] Have dinner with citizens once a week.

- [ ] Visit people in their homes.

- [ ] Talk to citizens on the phone.

- [ ] Live in many cities to learn about life in different places.

- [ ] Shop at stores where "regular" people shop.

- [ ] Do your laundry in a laundromat.

- [ ] Ride in a police car.

- [ ] Sit in the bleachers at a baseball game.

- [ ] Visit schools.

- [ ] _____

"Hi, this is the President calling."

Bonus: *Write to your mayor, Congressperson, or other leader and ask what that person does to stay in touch with the people.*

HOW TO BE PRESIDENT OF THE U.S.A.

MIND YOUR MANNERS

As President, you will often eat in public. Sometimes you'll dine with very important people (called VIPs) at fancy "state dinners."

You should know the correct way to use forks and other eating utensils. You must also know how to eat many types of food, from soups to souffles.

Try this: *Take the following quiz. The answers appear upside down at the bottom.*

	TRUE	FALSE
1. Use the large spoon for the soup.	☐	☐
2. When you eat the soup, slurp loudly to show how much you like it.	☐	☐
3. If gravy is left on your plate, you may wipe it up with a piece of bread.	☐	☐
4. Cut a big piece of fish or meat into many tiny chunks before eating any of it.	☐	☐
5. You may use your hands to eat some foods.	☐	☐
6. Don't talk when your mouth is full of food.	☐	☐

Bonus: *Pick a tricky-to-eat food, for example, spaghetti. Find out how to eat it by reading an etiquette book or by writing to the manners expert in your local paper.*

Answers: 1. True, 2. False, 3. False, 4. False, 5. True, 6. True

ANSWER YOUR MAIL

As President, you may receive more than 10,000 letters a day! Many letters will praise you. Others will say that you are doing an awful job. Some will offer ideas about improving the country. Others will ask questions like, "What's your favorite book?"

You won't have time to answer all of your mail, but there's help. In the Office of Correspondence, over 300 aides review the mail. Ready-made answers are used in most cases. A machine signs your name.

Try this: *Get ready to read a few of the letters that come to the White House each week. This way, you'll see what your fellow Americans are thinking about.*

Because your letters may be published one day, it's a good idea to practice your letter-reading and letter-writing skills.

Pretend you received the following letters. Choose one and write an answer for it.

Dear Mr. President,
*   I am nine years old and I want to be an astronaut. Do you have any plans for children to go on a space shuttle? Thank you very much.*
*   Sincerely,*
*   Laurie M.*

Dear Mr. President,
*   My mother just lost her job because her company went out of business. I am very worried and so is she. What are you doing about helping workers?*
*   Sincerely,*
*   Donald T.*

Dear Mr. President,
*   How much TV do you watch and what is your favorite show? Did you watch TV when you were a kid? Do you think television teaches you anything?*
*   Sincerely,*
*   Sandy P.*

Bonus: *Write a letter to the President and see what kind of response you get.*

★PRESIDENTIAL PEN PAL★

Shortly before election day in 1860, Abe Lincoln received the following letter. Grace Bedell, an 11-year-old, urged clean-shaven Abe to grow a beard.

Note: The wording, punctuation, and spelling in this typed version are the same as found in the original handwritten letter.

"NY

Westfield Chatauqua Co

"Oct 15, 1860

"Hon A B Lincoln

"Dear Sir

"My father has just come home from the fair and brought home your picture and Mr. Hamlin's. I am a little girl only eleven years old, but want you should be President of the United States very much so I hope you wont think me very bold to write to such a great man as you are. Have you any little girls about as large as I am if so give them my love and tell her to write to me, if you cannot answer this letter. I have got 4 brothers and part of them will vote for you anyway and if you will let your whiskers grow I will try and get the rest of them to vote for you you would look a great deal better for your face is so thin. All the ladies like whiskers and they would tease their husbands to vote for you and then you would be President. My father is agoing to vote for you to but I will try and get every one to vote for you that I can think that rail fence around your picture makes it look very pretty I have got a little baby sister she is nine weeks old and is just as cunning as can be. When you direct your letter direct it to Grace Bedell Westfield Chatauqua County New York.

"I must not write any more answer this letter right off Good bye.

"Grace Bedell"

Lincoln's friendly reply seems to say that the future President would not grow a beard.

However, photos taken at Lincoln's inauguration a few months later showed he had a full face of whiskers.

Private

Springfield Ills. Oct 19. 1860

Miss Grace Bedell

My dear little Miss.

Your very agreeable letter of the 15th is received—

I regret the necessity of saying I have no daughters—I have three sons—one seventeen, one nine, and one seven, years of age. They, with their mother, constitute my whole family.

As to the whiskers, having never worn any, do you not think people would call it a piece of silly affection if I were to begin it now—?

Your very sincere well-wisher

A. Lincoln

LEARN HOW TO TAKE A JOKE

No matter how hard you try to be a good President, some people won't like you. They may attack you in jokes, cartoons, songs, and skits. They may make fun of your ideas, your name, your friends, the way you talk, or the way you look.

To be a successful President, you need "thick skin." This means not letting mean jokes bother you. If you let yourself get angry, you may not be able to do your work. One way to handle insults is to remember the old jingle:

Sticks and stones
May break my bones
But names will never hurt me.

A more creative idea is to laugh at yourself before others do. This way, you'll be ready for almost anything they say about you.

Try this: *Draw a cartoon or write a story that teases you. It might make fun of things like*

- Your name

- Your hobbies

- Your pets

- Your habits

Bonus: *Read the newspaper. Look for letters and political cartoons that poke fun at the President or other leaders. Get into the leader's shoes. Ask yourself: "How would I feel about that? Could I take it?"*

PART 6

LEAVE OFFICE

Observe good faith and justice toward all nations; cultivate peace and harmony with all . . .

George Washington
Farewell Address
September 19, 1796

SHARE YOUR WISDOM

Starting with George Washington, Presidents have thought and written about many different topics, from books to taxes. They pick their words carefully, knowing that what they say may be read by present and future Americans.

Try this: *Write down what you think about each of the following topics. Then compare your ideas with what earlier Presidents have said.*

- Anger
- Books
- Education
- Freedom
- Honesty
- Human rights
- Hunger and poverty
- Knowledge
- Slavery
- Truth
- United Nations
- War and peace

Bonus: *Make a quotation book with your ideas on topics you care about.*

To furnish the means of acquiring knowledge is the greatest benefit that can be conferred upon mankind.

John Quincy Adams.

★PRESIDENTIAL QUOTE BOOK★

Anger

When angry, count ten before you speak; if very angry, a hundred.
—Thomas Jefferson

Books

I cannot live without books.
—Thomas Jefferson

Education

Upon the subject of education . . . I can only say that I view it as the most important subject which we as a people may be engaged in.
—Abraham Lincoln

Freedom

Those who deny freedom to others deserve it not for themselves, and, under a just God, cannot long retain it.
—Abraham Lincoln

Honesty

The whole of government consists in the art of being honest.
—Thomas Jefferson

Human Rights

We look forward to a world founded upon four essential human freedoms. The first is freedom of speech and expression everywhere in the world. The second is freedom of every person to worship God in his own way, everywhere in the world. The third is freedom from want . . . The fourth is freedom from fear . . .
—Franklin Roosevelt

Hunger and Poverty

No one can worship God or love his neighbor on an empty stomach.
—Woodrow Wilson

Knowledge

There is nothing which can better deserve our patronage than the promotion of science and literature. Knowledge is in every country the surest basis of happiness.
—George Washington

Slavery

If slavery is not wrong, nothing is wrong.
—Abraham Lincoln

Truth

I am a firm believer in the people. If given the truth, they can be depended upon to meet any national crisis. The great point is to bring them the real facts.
—Abraham Lincoln

United Nations

I believe that our Great Maker is preparing the world, in His own good time, to become one nation, speaking one language . . . when armies and navies will no longer be required.
—Ulysses S. Grant

War and Peace

If we do not abolish war on this earth, then surely, one day, war will abolish us from the earth.
—Harry S. Truman

Every gun that is made, every warship launched, every rocket fired, signifies in the final sense a theft from those who hunger and are not fed, those who are cold and are not clothed. This world in arms is not spending money alone. It is spending the sweat of its laborers, the genius of its scientists, the houses of its children.
—Dwight D. Eisenhower

GET A JOB

Of the first 40 Presidents, eight died in office. Others retired to a life of quiet. But many spent their last years hard at work. For example, Ulysses Grant, who needed money to pay off debts, wrote a best-selling book about his life. Andrew Johnson was elected to the Senate.

After you serve as President, you'll probably be offered many kinds of jobs. Are there some that you think an ex-President shouldn't take?

Try this: *Tell whether you think a retired President should do the following jobs. Add your own ideas for after-White House work.*

	OK	NOT OK
1. Sell products in TV commercials.	☐	☐
2. Become a movie star.	☐	☐
3. Write a book on being President.	☐	☐
4. Become a teacher.	☐	☐
5. Sell products to the government.	☐	☐
6. Work for foreign countries.	☐	☐
7. _____	☐	☐
8. _____	☐	☐

Bonus: *Take a poll. Ask people what jobs they think a retired President should and should not do. Write an article about what you learn for your school or town paper.*

What Some Retired Presidents Did

✓ George Washington farmed.

✓ Grover Cleveland took four years off, ran for President, and was reelected.

✓ Theodore Roosevelt hunted big game.

✓ William Taft became Chief Justice of the Supreme Court.

✓ Richard Nixon practiced law.

✓ Jimmy Carter helped other nations develop democratic governments.

✓ Ronald Reagan gave speeches in the United States and abroad.

WRITE YOUR LEGEND

In 1800, Mason ("Parson") Weems wrote the first presidential biography: *The Life and Memorable Actions of George Washington.* The book was so popular, Parson Weems added more stories, including the cherry tree legend. As one of the nation's most popular tales, it taught Americans to value honesty.

Step 1. Pick a quality that you value in yourself, for example, your intelligence, humor, or energy.

Step 2. Think of a setting in which you might use that quality, for example, at school, in a club, or at home.

Step 3. When writing your story, try to include easy-to-remember dialogue. An example is Parson Weems' famous line: "I can't tell a lie."

Step 4. If possible, include an object (like George Washington's hatchet) in the story. Your legend might feature an item like a mountain bike or a Walkman.

Try this: *Do your best to be the kind of President Americans will want to remember a hundred or a thousand years from now.*

Because you can't be sure that someone like Parson Weems will make up a wonderful legend about you, write one yourself.

The Cherry Tree Legend

One day George Washington received a hatchet as a gift. He was so eager to use it that he cut down one of his father's cherry trees.

When his father came out of the house and saw that the tree had been cut down, he asked George about it.

"I can't tell a lie, pa; you know I can't tell a lie. I did it with my hatchet."

"Run to my arms, you dearest boy," cried his father; "run to my arms; glad am I, George, that you killed my tree, for you have paid me a thousandfold. Such an act of heroism in my son is worth more than a thousand trees, though blossomed with silver, and their fruits of purest gold."

BE REMEMBERED

A lot can happen while you are President. You may launch dozens of projects, work on hundreds of laws, and help solve countless problems.

But in the end, you'll probably be remembered for how you handled just one or two big tasks.

For example, if the United States goes to war while you're President, history books may focus on your military leadership. Other big achievements may be forgotten.

Try this: *While you won't be able to control what happens during your years in office, you might find it useful to imagine how you want to be remembered. For example, if you care about education, you might hope that people in the future will recall you as the "Education President."*

Choose two or three nicknames that could stand for your presidency. Then, pick one and tell why it's the most important.

- [ ] The Arts President
- [ ] The Children's President
- [ ] The Civil Rights President
- [ ] The Education President
- [ ] The Environment President
- [ ] The Family President
- [ ] The Fun President
- [ ] The Military President
- [ ] The Parks President
- [ ] The Peace President
- [ ] The Poverty-reducing President
- [ ] The Science President
- [ ] The Trade-increasing President
- [ ] The Transportation President
- [ ] _____

Presidential Nicknames

Father of the Country: George Washington

Friend of the People: Thomas Jefferson

Father of the Smithsonian: John Q. Adams

Do Nothing President: James Buchanan

The Great Emancipator: Abraham Lincoln

Sir Veto: Andrew Johnson

Trust Buster: Theodore Roosevelt

Puritan President: Calvin Coolidge

Great Humanitarian: Franklin Roosevelt

Mr. Nice Guy: Gerald Ford

Great Communicator: Ronald Reagan

Bonus: *What nickname would you use for your life to this point? Explain it.*

PRESIDENTS REMEMBERED

George Washington
1789-1793, 1793-1797

John Adams
1797-1801

Thomas Jefferson
1801-1805, 1805-1809

James Madison
1809-1813, 1813-1817

James Monroe
1817-1821, 1821-1825

John Q. Adams
1825-1829

Andrew Jackson
1829-1833, 1833-1837

Martin Van Buren
1837-1841

William H. Harrison
1841, died in office

John Tyler
1841-1845

James K. Polk
1845-1849

Zachary Taylor
1849-1850

Millard Fillmore
1850-1853

Franklin Pierce
1853-1857

James Buchanan
1857-1861

Abraham Lincoln
1861-1865,
1865, died in office

Andrew Johnson
1865-1869

Ulysses S. Grant
1869-1873, 1873-1877

Rutherford B. Hayes
1877-1881

James A. Garfield
1881, died in office

PRESIDENTS REMEMBERED

Chester A. Arthur
1881-1885

Grover Cleveland
1885-1889, 1893-1897

Benjamin Harrison
1889-1893

William McKinley
1897-1901,
1901, died in office

Theodore Roosevelt
1901-1905, 1905-1909

William H. Taft
1909-1913

Woodrow Wilson
1913-1917, 1917-1921

Warren G. Harding
1921-1923, died in office

Calvin Coolidge
1923-1925, 1925-1929

Herbert Hoover
1929-1933

Franklin D. Roosevelt
1933-1937, 1937-1941, 1941-1945
1945, died in office

Harry S. Truman
1945-1949, 1949-1953

Dwight D. Eisenhower
1953-1957, 1957-1961

John F. Kennedy
1961-1963, died in office

Lyndon B. Johnson
1963-1965, 1965-1969

Richard M. Nixon
1969-1973, 1973-1974 resigned

Gerald R. Ford
1974-1977

James E. Carter, Jr.
1977-1981

Ronald W. Reagan
1981-1985, 1985-1989

George Bush
1989-

HOW TO BE PRESIDENT OF THE U.S.A.

READING LIST

Note: In addition to the following books, *The World Almanac*, updated yearly, is a rich source for facts about America, the Constitution, and the presidency.

CONSTITUTION OF THE UNITED STATES

If You Were There When They Signed the Constitution by Elizabeth Levy (Scholastic, 1987). Tells why the Constitution is called a "miracle."

Shh! We're Writing the Constitution by Jean Fritz (Putnam's, 1987). Shows how Madison, Franklin, and others created a new nation.

We the People by Peter Spier (Doubleday, 1987). Uses pictures to explain Constitutional phrases, such as "promote the general Welfare."

DEFENSE

The National Defense System by Stephen Goode (Franklin Watts, 1977). Covers issues every Commander in Chief must grasp.

JUSTICE

The Supreme Court by Ann Weiss (Enslow, 1987). Discusses federal and state legal systems.

LETTER WRITING

A Treasury of Great American Letters by C. Hurd (Hawthorn, 1961). Traces history through letters by Columbus, Abigail Adams, George Washington Carver, Susan B. Anthony, and others.

MONEY

Money by Harry Neal (Messner, 1967). Describes the history of money and its role in trade.

PRESIDENTS AND THE PRESIDENCY

The American Presidency by Ann Weiss (Messner, 1976). Describes the President's job, with facts about inaugurations, politics, Congress, and separation of powers.

Lincoln: a Photobiography by Russell Freedman (Clarion, 1987). Captures Lincoln in photos.

Franklin Delano Roosevelt by Russell Freedman (Clarion, 1990). Follows the life of F.D.R. from birth to the White House.

The Look-It-Up Book of Presidents by Wyatt Blassingame (Random House, 1988). Tells about the Presidents.

The World Almanac of Presidential Facts by Lu Paletta and Fred Worth (World Almanac, 1988). Gives firsts, mottoes, namesakes, nicknames, favorites, and unusual lists, for example, "All the Presidents Born in a Log Cabin."

SONGS

Songs America Voted By by Irwin Silver (Stackpole, 1971). Moves from "God Save Great Washington" (melody: "America") to JFK's "Everyone is Voting for Jack" (melody: "High Hopes").

Music for Patriots, Politicians, and Presidents by Vera Brodsky Lawrence (Macmillan, 1975). Has marches, ballads, campaign songs, and the "Hail to the Chief" story.

SPEECHES

A Treasury of Great American Speeches by C. Hurd (Hawthorn, 1959). Honors the words of such figures as Sam Adams, Ben Franklin, George Washington, Mark Twain, Booker T. Washington, Emma Goldman, and Charles Lindbergh.

UNITED NATIONS

The United Nations from A to Z by Nancy Parker (Dodd, Mead, 1985). Features maps, drawings, and diagrams.

WASHINGTON, D.C.

A Kid's Guide to Washington, D.C. (Harcourt, 1989). Offers maps, photos, drawings, quizzes, and intriguing facts.

WHITE HOUSE

How the White House Really Works by George Sullivan (Dutton, 1989). Explores every nook and cranny from the Oval Office to the laundry.

The White House by Leonard Fisher (Holiday House, 1989). Tells the history of a world-famous building.

PRESIDENTIAL ADDRESS BOOK

GENERAL

Congress/Capitol
Washington, D.C. 20515

Federal Bureau of Investigation (F.B.I.)
Pennsylvania Ave. NW
Washington, D.C 20535

Government Printing Office
710 N. Capitol St.
Washington, D.C. 20401

House of Representatives
Capitol Building
Washington, D.C. 20515

Library of Congress
101 Independence Ave. SE
Washington, D.C. 20540

National Aeronautics & Space Administration (NASA)
600 Independence Ave. SW
Washington, D.C. 20546

National Archives
7th & Pennsylvania Ave. NW
Washington, D.C. 20408

Organization of the American States
Constitution Ave. & 17th St. NW
Washington, D.C. 20230

Pentagon
Arlington, Virginia 20301

Senate Office Building
Washington, D.C. 20510

Supreme Court
One 1st St. NE
Washington, D.C. 20543

United Nations
New York, New York 10017

White House
1600 Pennsylvania Ave.
Washington, D.C. 20500
202-456-1414

PRESIDENTIAL LIBRARIES

Jimmy Carter Library
One Copenhill
Atlanta, Georgia 30307-1498
404-331-3942

Dwight Eisenhower Center
S.E. Fourth St.
Abilene, Kansas 67410
913-263-4751

Gerald Ford Library
1000 Beal Ave.
Ann Arbor, Michigan 48109-2114
313-668-2218

Rutherford Hayes Library
1337 Hayes Ave.
Fremont, Ohio 43420-2796
419-332-2081

Herbert Hoover Library
West Branch, Iowa 52358
319-643-5301

Lyndon Johnson Library & Museum
2313 Red River
Austin, Texas 78705-5702
512-482-5137

John Kennedy Library
Columbia Point
Boston, Massachusetts 02125
617-929-4554

Richard Nixon Library
18001 Yorba Linda Blvd.
Yorba Linda, California 92686
714-993-3393

Ronald Reagan Library
40 Presidential Dr.
Simi Valley, California 93065
805-522-8444

Franklin D. Roosevelt Library
511 Albany Post Rd.
Hyde Park, New York 12538
914-229-8114

Harry S. Truman Library
24 Highway & Delaware
Independence, Missouri 64050
816-833-1400

GLOSSARY

Every President should understand the following words.

Amendment to the Constitution: a change made to the highest law of the land; for example, Amendment XIII abolished (ended) slavery

Balance of power: dividing government into branches (parts) so that no person or group has total control

Bill of Rights: the Constitution's first 10 Amendments, which protect the rights of people and the states

Budget: a plan to balance income from taxes with outgo (payments) for roads and other services

Cabinet: a group of top Presidential advisers

Capital: the home city of government, Washington, D.C.

Capitol: the building where Congress meets to write laws

Civil rights: freedoms guaranteed by the Bill of Rights and related Amendments (13th, 14th, 15th, 19th)

Congress: the legislative (law-making) branch of government; it has two parts, the Senate and the House of Representatives

Constitution: the nation's supreme (most important) law; it tells how the government works

Debt: money that is owed; the government's debt is owed to people or groups who buy government bonds

Economy: the way a nation creates and shares wealth (cars, clothing, haircuts, plumbing, schools, etc.)

Executive: a leader or manager; the President is the chief executive of the United States government

Federal: whatever has to do with the central (U.S.) government; for example, federal courts deal with laws made by Congress

House of Representatives: the branch of Congress based on population; states with more people have more Representatives than states with few people; members of the House are elected for two years

Politics: debating, compromising, and other activities to make laws or reach other goals in government

President-elect: the winner of the presidential election before he or she takes office

Senate: the branch of Congress based on representing the states; each state sends two Senators to the Senate for six-year terms

Speaker of the House: the person who leads the majority party in the House of Representatives

Supreme Court: the nation's highest court; its nine members can cancel laws and presidential actions that go against the Constitution

Tax: a payment made to support the government

Veto: the President's refusal to sign a bill and make it a law

INDEX